HOW TO START A BUSINESS: 12 IDEAS FOR A SUCCESSFUL BUSINESS

by Daniel M. Hill

www.chin-life.com

All rights reserved. No part of this publication may be reproduced, distributed, or transmitted in any form or by any means, including photocopying, recording, or other electronic or mechanical methods, without the prior written permission of the publisher, except in the case of brief quotations embodied in critical reviews and certain other noncommercial uses permitted by copyright law. For permission requests, write to the publisher, addressed "Attention: Permissions Coordinator," at the address below.

info@chin-life.com

Copyright © 2017 by Chin Life Publishing

TABLE OF CONTENT
by Daniel M. Hill

INTRODUCE

CHAPTER 1. BUSINESS ON REPAIR AND RESTORATION

CHAPTER 2. BECOME THE COORDINATOR OF EVENTS (BIRTHDAYS, WEDDINGS, CORPORATE PARTIES)

CHAPTER 3. BECOME A TUTOR (MUSIC, DRAWING, LANGUAGES, SCHOOL SUBJECTS), IF YOU HAVE ANY SKILLS IN THIS

CHAPTER 4. TAKE UP FREELANCING (DESIGN, PHOTOGRAPHER, TRANSLATION OF TEXTS, COPYWRITING, DEVELOPING OF WEBSITES)

CHAPTER 5. BECOME AN INTERNET MARKETER (INSTAGRAM, GOOGLE ADWORDS, FACEBOOK). IT'S NOT SO DIFFICULT TO LEARN

CHAPTER 6. BECOME A YOUTUBE BLOGGER IN AN AREA THAT YOU KNOW WELL (WHERE YOU ARE A PROFESSIONAL)

CHAPTER 7. OPEN THE TRUCK WITH FOOD AND DRINKS (COFEE). WITH THE SUBSEQUENT GROWTH OF A NUMBER OF TRUCK

CHAPTER 8. OPEN A VISITING BUSINESS IN THE FIELD OF BEAUTY (MANICURE, HAIRSTYLES, PEDICURE, EYEBROWS)

CHAPTER 9. WALK WITH DOGS, OR TAKE THEM TO YOURSELF FOR OVEREXPOSURE (OR ANY OTHER ANIMALS)

CHAPTER 10. BECOME A NURSE FOR CHILDREN (NANNY, BABYSITTER)

CHAPTER 11. LEASE YOOUR FREE PROPERTY FOR RENT

CHAPTER 12. COOK SWEETS AT HOME. SELL VIA THE INTERNET

CONCLUSION

INTRODUCE

At the first blush, everyone can say that starting a business without start-up capital is a real fantasy. In turn, the presence of large initial investment is a common form of stereotypes, sort of usual patterned thinking. Those people, who are confident about the impossibility of this, are bright representatives of business blindness owners - the lack or inability to see money, when they can simply take them, while reducing their costs to almost zero. Many entrepreneurs, who have an extensive experience in international and domestic business, argue that any private business has the right to exist, if its creator is laid out 100%. This is the most important point of this article. Therefore, here are some tips, which can help you to become more self-confident about starting your own business and succeed in this.

Business is like a sport. So your inner attitude and mental attitude is very important in this case. If you are mentally prepared for the upcoming difficulties, ups and downs, then your business will last a long time. If you do not have money, but you decide to start your own business, then be ready for a long journey. With money everything is easier, but without them ... well, you get it☺

CHAPTER 1. BUSINESS ON REPAIR AND RESTORATION

In 90% of cases, it's possible to start business without money only on services. This is logical, since you earn on your own. With goods it happens so rarely, because in most cases the goods need to be purchased, and these are investments.

So one of business types is repair and restoration of bicycles. If you know to do anything from this

If you once were, and maybe still being a bicyclist, then you probably should know and fully understand how important it is that the "iron horse" to be always in good condition. At the same time, there are not so many really good bicycle masters who know how to correctly inspect and repair any of the failures that a bicycle. It is this fact that gives the basis for starting a business of repair and maintenance of bicycles. The whole essence of this type of business boils down to the opening of a bike shop, a service for the repair and maintenance of bicycles, where the entire range of services will be provided, which are directly related to the repair of bicycles and their preventive technical inspection. It can be like the usual replacement of the chain, the elimination of a puncture in the tire or the adjustment of the G8, and other services, up to the harvesting and sale of bike parts and accessories for them.

To start this business does not require large monetary investments, and the monthly costs for its support will be minimal. The growing consumer demand for these types of services, as the number of bicycles increases every year, which also contributes to the increased demand for their repair. The schedule of work is flexible, full or part-time. Skills for repairing bicycles, as well as knowledge for managing commercial activities are small, they can be learned in a fairly short time. You can get extra profit from the sale of spare parts for bicycles, a variety of accessories (Velosoo, bike computer) and so on. You can also highlight several points for the directions of the bike shop, which can function separately or together. It can be Current or urgent repairs, which can be broken down into price categories (depending on the complexity of the repair and the time spent); sale of any bike spare parts and accessories; carrying out maintenance at the beginning of the driving season cycling (pumping wheel, checking the brakes, lubrication); in the presence of an appropriate premises, it's possible to provide customer with bicycle storage services outside the season for a certain subscription fee.

After the opening of the bicycle repair shop, first of all, it's desirable to make business cards and leaflets that you need to leave in bicycle shops and sports shops, also give out your business cards to friends and acquaintances, ask them to advertise your undertaking to others. It is also necessary to advertise in different newspapers, and post relevant advertisements on the streets. A simple arithmetic calculation shows that you spend quite a bit (print ads and business cards, as well as posting in newspapers), but get a lot of publicity. In addition to these advertising moves, you can also engage in the promotion of your services on the Internet, however, it will take quite some time, however, as the advance itself in this direction will require more significant investments.

However, using your own website, you will be able to provide users with the most complete information about their work (photos and video materials), as well as promptly inform them about various changes, discounts and share that you will eventually arrange. If we talk about price policy in more detail, then in this issue, of course, it is difficult to determine, because it will increasingly depend on the region in which you live and the places where you will open your bicycle repair business.

Since, people started thinking about their own health, exercise and sport, changing from car seats to bicycle seats, the business of bicycle repair is extremely promising and modern.

Repair and restoration of plumbing equipment

In a modern metropolis, a business based on the provision of plumbing services is essentially bottomless. You can judge for yourself. How many houses are in the modern city? How many apartments in them, and how many will be put into use? There is a huge number, and every apartment has plumbing, which sooner or later goes out of order and requires a planned replacement. Today, not so many people have the necessary skills, tools that you can buy at the store and enough time to repair yourself on your own, and so they turn to the masters. The number of potential customers is so great that alone you cannot master the fulfillment of all orders.

The best option would be to create a small plumbing service company, which will have a whole staff of masters. In addition to minor scheduled repairs, it is advisable to include in the list of services provided and complete replacement of all plumbing, while providing services for the acquisition and delivery of all necessary things. With this scheme, your income should increase not from the cost of services, but from the number of customers, so you need to make prices for services lower than for plumbers who work alone. In addition, customers' trust can be won if you are on call 24 hours a day, providing services at any time of the day or night. After all, it's possible to break the pipe at any time, especially in old houses.

This business can bring a very good income. However, even if you act exclusively as an organizer and leader, you still have to understand the plumbing. The quality of the services provided by your firm will directly depend on your competence. Although today the market of sanitary services is far from empty and there is a lot of competition, plumbers will always work. Here is an indicative list of plumbing services:

- Dismantling of the toilet;
- dismantling the sink;
- dismantling the heated towel rail;
- removing the bathtub;
- installing the bathtub;
- installing the bathtub;
- installing the bathtub with the hydro-massage;
- installing the toilet and washbasin;
- installing the sink in the kitchen;
- installing the heated towel rail;
- installing the water heater;
- installation of a water meter;
- installation of water filters for coarse cleaning;
- installation of a fine filter with rinsing;
- installation of automatic water purification filter;
- installation of a reducer;
- dismantling of the radiator;
- installation of a radiator;
- cutting of the cranes into the riser;
- constriction of the riser;
- installation and connection of the circulating pump;
- riser with lowering the outlet into the slab;
- displacement of the heating pipes from the riser to the radiator in the wall with grinding;
- replacement of the heating pipe (riser);

- installation of the heating pipe in the wall (riser);
- installation of the shower rod;
- installation and connection of the washing machine;
- installation and connection of dishwasher;
- installation of a shower cabin;
- installation of an electric towel warmer;
- Painting of heating pipes.

Having compiled the table it's necessary to analyze the prices of competitors, calculate the cost of work and profit from each position, and calculate the minimum earnings of a specialist. Depending on the capacity of the market, determine the number of employees. It's worth of noting that when setting the price, when installing expensive equipment, the percentage of the cost of the installed items is added to the basic cost of sanitary services. Also, the price can be affected by repairs, which are already made in the bathroom. After all, there is a risk of damage to material assets, the cost of which in this case will need to be reimbursed.

Repair and restoration of phones with the subsequent resale

Workshops for the repair of cell phones, smart phones and communicators are met at every step, but as a rule, they are filled with orders, and in a rare workshop you will be offered urgent repairs. A small workshop can be placed in front of the supermarket ticket offices, in the underground passage or in the basement of a residential building. Plus, you can arrange only the point of reception, and repair the phones at home or in the garage. In this case, the cost of rent is reduced in two-three times: only space for a chair and a table, a signboard, tablets with a schedule of work and a price list – these are those things which will be needed. If you decide to rent a small room in the basement of an apartment house, converted for trade and services, you will probably need to make repairs. In this case it will be enough to do only cosmetic repairs, which will significantly reduce financial costs.

You don't have to receive any certificates, fill complicated forms of documents and even put a cash register. As any enterprise in the service sector, the workshop must specify the hours of work, compile a price list and design a "consumer corner" - a booth where a complaint book and rules for the provision of services to the public will be placed.

If you can repair phones by yourself, you will only need one shift worker. You will have to hire a receptionist-administrator, who will issue receipts and answer calls. With an increase of the number of employees, costs will also increase. It will be necessary to pay salaries, taxes and equip jobs. But the profit, of course, increases. In addition, during the reporting period, the accountant will need services.

Advertising is the engine of everything in our information age. Therefore, it's very important a starting entrepreneur to declare himself correctly. Especially if we take into account the fact that in the sphere of repair of smart phones and mobile phones in big cities, there is quite a lot of competition. A signboard, a banner, an advertising pillar - there are many ways to declare themselves, it is better to use them in a complex. It's also nice to make business cards right away. Although, usual ways of advertising in this business give a small return. It is strongly recommended that you create a service center site and promote it on the Internet. Similarly, the bulk of advertising should be concentrated on the open spaces of the network. You can save on promotion or site creation, if you can do it yourself or someone from your employees.

Repair and restoration of boats

There are many people who own a boat and a business related to boats such as repair is a lucrative business. Boats are a part of earth's history and considered as something that has been with men since time immemorial. Any boat owner will at one point in the live of his/her boat will have the need for repair. Boat repair business can truly be a rewarding business. You will be given the opportunity to serve your clients to the best of your capacity plus you will also be given the opportunity to use the boat yourself while testing it after the repair.

Though a boat repair business will more likely require you to set up your business in an area near the water still you will have to study the competition of the business. What can you offer to your clients that will make you stand out from the rest of the boat repair businesses in your area? Boats like cars need maintenance and repairs as well. Getting into this business unprepared will most likely fail and you loose your hard earned money. Of course there will ups and downs in any business venture but the key factor to success is superior knowledge of the business. Learn all the peripherals about boat repair. This is one of the factors to your success.

State of the art equipment is a come on when it comes to boat repairs. You will have the need to invest in equipment and tools that you will need in your business. Though most of these equipment and tools can be costly you will more likely to earn them back once you have acquired a steady flow of customers. You will just have to maintain an excellent relationship with your clients.

Getting certified in boat repairs will be your advantage over the others who does business purely by experience. The more certifications you can hang on the wall of your office the more you can attract more customers. Customers who walk in your office may not ask for it but the certifications on your wall will speak for you how capable you are in the business. Of course your space is a must in dealing with your customers. Set up an office near the waters for accessibility to your customers. It doesn't have to be big, just enough for you to have a space where you can discuss business with your clients and storage area for your equipment and tools. You will require a few staff to help you out with your business. Hire the most competent staff, preferably somebody whose education and knowledge of the business is excellent as yours.

Repair and restoration of small engines

Mechanically inclined entrepreneurs have an opportunity to make fantastic full- or part-time cash repairing outdoor power equipment and small engines, right from a fully equipped home based workshop, or from a small commercial storefront. Even though if you do not have previous small-engine repair experience, there are numerous schools offering in-class and correspondence small-engine repair training, such as the one listed below. The list of equipment you can repair is almost unlimited: lawn mowers, outboard motors, gas trimmers, lawn tractors, snowmobiles, snow blowers, leaf blowers, and chainsaws are only the tip of the iceberg. There are additional revenue sources as well. The first is to establish a certified-warranty repair depot for outdoor power-equipment manufacturers. The second is to buy secondhand outdoor power equipment in need of repairs at dirt-cheap prices, fix it, and sell it for a profit right from your shop. And the third additional revenue source is to rent outdoor power equipment and tools to local homeowners and contractors. Combine the three with the repair side of the business and you could easily generate in excess of $100,000 per year in sales.

So if you spend your spare time repairing or revving up the engine parts, you could build a successful business repairing small engines. Small engines produce less than 25 horsepower and are often gas powered. In fact, people who repaired small engines used to be called small engine mechanics. With the increase in gas-powered equipment, many in the profession now refer to themselves as Outdoor Power Equipment Technicians. If you imagine the insides of your neighbor's garage, you'll probably see at least several machines using small engines. You can almost always find a lawn mower engine or a tractor engine. You can also find snow blowers, trimmers, and leaf blowers, all using small engines. Small engines are found from the garage as well. Outboard motors, portable generators and pressure washers.

It helps if you already are comfortable working with machines – taking them apart, putting them back together and troubleshooting. A background in engineering or mechanics is extremely useful. However, if you have the interest but not the experience, enroll in a small engine repair school. Many schools offer online training, and trade schools offer onsite training. Although it is not required, you can also get certified as a technician. The Outdoor Power Equipment Engine Service Association (opeesa.com) offers a certification process they believe will add to your credentials.

You will need a work area, usually a well-lit, well-ventilated garage, with a good set of tools. Depending on the season that you start, you can market your repairs to the types of machines currently in use, or about to be in use. For example, in late winter, begin advertising your lawn equipment repair service, and continue until autumn. In spring, advertise for outboard motor and motorcycle repair. In fall, advertise for snow blower repair – you see the trend. You can put ads online at craigslist.org, and small ads in local and free newspapers. Periodically distribute flyers to neighborhoods where people do their own yard work, and are likely to have equipment. Once customers come in for repairs, offer a maintenance plan and a service guarantee.

In addition to getting jobs from individuals, you can also work with businesses. Landscapers have lawn care equipment, businesses use pressure washers and construction companies use portable generators—all with small engines. Contact the businesses periodically so the next time they have an engine problem, they think of coming back to your small engine repair business.

Plus, to making repairs, you can also stock and sell supplies like common lawn mower parts. Or you can buy components needing repair for a low price, fix them and sell them for a profit. You can also become a certified warranty repair center for particular equipment. With technical experience and a little marketing, you can rev up a profitable small engine repair business.

Building repair and restoration of premises (floor, windows)

Whatever surprises await us in the political and economic life of the country; there are three things, which will always remain unchanged: these are products, clothing, and housing. Today in any relatively large city there are many construction projects. The construction of multi-storey houses almost never stops, but, as you know, builders are not engaged in interior decoration, and the buyer of the new building gets an apartment in which you still need to make a full repair. And in many already residential apartments' construction and finishing work is constantly required. It's rarely when person starts repairs on his own; therefore, the services of repair and construction brigades are in great demand on the market. These specialists of a wide profile offer their customers' fast execution of tasks, the cost of their services can be different depending on the level and popularity of the team, but in any city it is not difficult to find builders and repairmen.

This niche of business is quite densely occupied, because it does not require serious investments, and a person with a construction education, if he wants to do his own business, will certainly choose not to open a full-fledged construction company. The level of competition in this direction is very high, and it is quite difficult to enter the market for a beginner, he does not have a reputation and a well-known name, while many construction teams already have a well-developed clientele. On the other hand, residents of new buildings, people who first encountered the need for finishing works, try to find out information about repair and construction teams in general sources, for example, on the Internet, where the young company has a chance to interest its client with a more profitable service offer, and not Known name.

In this regard, even a beginner company can take its place, but for this you will have to constantly engage in a marketing campaign and earn a positive reputation. On the first stages, a small number of orders can be justified economically, but later the organization should develop, and in order to survive on this market, you need to offer your customers truly high-quality services without hackwork. It is also worth of noting that a relatively large number of repair construction crews today are offering low-quality services, they are builders who finish in their spare time and therefore rarely care about good work, but offers the customer a low cost and short terms, that attracts consumers in a special way. These are those brigades that bypass with random orders, who may not have very good reviews in the market, but at the same time they survive due to their connections and externally favorable conditions. Thus, a novice must eventually offer competitive conditions, but also seek to set their prices below average.

The repair and construction team offers a wide range of services, ranging from simple cosmetic finishing of the walls to the laying of communications. In order to start your own business, you need to register as a subject of entrepreneurial activity, and in case of a small company, it makes sense to choose the form of individual entrepreneurship, because it takes less time, requires and serious reporting, and as a result, the registration costs a bit cheaper. If there is a need to formalize a legal entity, the form of a limited liability company is preferable, because in this case, as in the case of individual entrepreneurship, a simplified system of taxation will be available. If there is a need to formalize a legal entity, the form of a limited liability company is preferable, because in this case, as in the case of individual entrepreneurship, a simplified system of taxation will be available.

Currently, special construction licenses are not required, but for legal business it is necessary to join a self-regulating organization (SRO) for construction. In this regard, it is impossible to accurately name the amount of necessary contributions of the entry fee and other conditions for accepting newcomers to a self-regulatory organization, because each of them sets its own conditions and requirements. Work without joining the SRO is strictly prohibited, but it has some of its advantages. For example, in a self-regulatory organization, information may appear that it will transmit to its members. Also there appears information about state grants and contests that can be used. In any case, the entrepreneur now does not need to constantly apply to state authorities and engage in his activities under the supervision of the governing bodies. SRO issues admission to work, and although it requires its members to fulfill all the conditions set, less demanding.

Next, you need to think about finding a room, while seriously considering the option of a general lack of its own office and representation. If the budget is limited, then it is possible to conduct all negotiations with their customers at their home, all the more, this will allow to combine negotiations with the evaluation and calculation of the cost of work. Customers rarely judge a company by its office, because it is much more convenient for them when the brigade immediately arrives at the place and there is no need to go somewhere. In this regard, you can save a lot on renting premises in the first months of work, especially when there is still only a small number of orders, and the company for many days without work.

However, later you will have to think about your own office, because a developing company increases the range of services provided, its service level rises, and it can not do without its own representation. To do this, it's better to look for a room in the area of large-scale construction, for example, in a new block under construction, which will soon be delivered, and apartments will begin to be sold. Of course, sooner or later the quarter will be completely settled, and the demand for finishing works will gradually fall, but by that time the company will have a good reputation that will allow it to work throughout the city, and in the extreme case it should be able to move to the new quarter. Therefore, if the firm has not yet gained wide popularity, it is worth renting small offices with the possibility of rapid relocation.

It should be noted that it's better to start a repair and construction business for an entrepreneur who himself understands repair and construction, but at the same time has a higher professional education and sufficient experience to personally supervise the construction or repair process. Of course, complex projects require the involvement of a large number of people, including additional management personnel, but it's preferable for an entrepreneur to personally manage the work of his employees. In other words, the businessman himself must act directly at the site, otherwise the brigade with his own foreman does not need to work for a third-party company, because, having received the object, she will strive to leave all the profits to herself. It follows that the brigade with the foreman involved from the side with a high probability will begin to engage in the provision of its services bypassing the employing firm, without caring about the reputation and image of the latter.

In this regard, the repair and construction business can be recommended to those people who can independently manage the construction and repair process and who want to organize their own business, entrepreneurs who are far from building, it is better to choose some other direction of their activities, and if there is a huge Desire or prospects to engage in this particular area, it is necessary to study the main points of this business, but also constantly monitor the work of its employees.

The deciding factor in such an undertaking will be the selection of their own team. It is people who depend on the quality and speed of the work, so this issue should be approached very carefully. In the labor market, repairers and builders can easily be found today, but not always they will be qualified employees, responsible and not seeking to deceive employers or clients. This is one of the reasons why it is recommended to perform the work of a superintendent on your own or at least constantly monitor the work of your team. Certainly, it will take a long time before you can find really honest and skilled workers, and at first will have to cooperate with different people.

Most often today people are looking for employees of interior decoration on the advice of friends and acquaintances, those potential clients who cannot ask for advice or get a recommendation, seek information primarily on the Internet. Therefore, you need to seriously think about creating your own website, which will become an important information and advertising platform for the company.

The cost of creating and promoting a site can be very significant, depending on the subject matter, the content of the site and the level of competition. However, it is through the Internet today you can find the largest number of customers, because the site immediately offers a list of prices, a list of services and all working conditions. The cost of the work of the repair and construction brigade varies depending on the complexity, and among the professionals there is selection of several repair groups.

The most time-consuming, energy-consuming and time-consuming work can cost customers several times more. Therefore, such a business is beneficial in the event that there are a large number of orders, but a significant disadvantage of this business is its seasonality, because in the cold season almost no one is engaged in repair. In connection with this repair and finishing business to deal with some other, if, of course, there is a need to receive cash all year round.

Repair and restoration of rare furniture

Stripping, sanding and finishing chairs, tables and heirlooms - the fundamentals of any furniture refinishing business – are a kind of an art. Refinishing furniture might also involve reupholstering - an additional skill that's good to have for this home business. Starting a furniture refinishing business is not something you should take up on the fly - either you already have the skills or you must learn through classes or an apprenticeship. Seasoned pros can expand into reselling antique furniture they've purchased at flea markets or from private dealers. Furniture refinishing often thrives in tough times when people are determined to spruce up what they already have rather than buy new.

There are some things you will definitely need to do before starting such business:

- Professional before-and-after photos of work you've done, even if it's on your own furniture or inexpensive test pieces you might find at a garage sale or flea market – the improvements should be dramatic enough to highlight your skills.

- Business cards, print and online advertising, vehicle signage – ideally on a van or truck -- and a website to promote your business.

- Furniture refinishing equipment and supplies, including strippers and sanding tools.

- A well-ventilated workspace and safety equipment to help you avoid inhaling toxic chemical fumes.

- Relationships with antique dealers, flea markets and collectors to spread word of your services and promote repeat business.

- Bookkeeping skills - consider hiring an accountant if you don't have them.

Advantages of furniture business are obvious. As this can be the ideal career for do-it-yourselfers and those who love to worth with their hands. Antique lovers will flock to your door because they tend to prefer custom refinishing to factory refinishing. You can set your own hours, stripping and sanding into the predawn hours if you're a night owl, although pickup and delivery times must conform to your customers' timetables. If you work out of your own home – maybe your garage -- overhead won't be steep after you purchase the initial necessary equipment.

But there are also some disadvantages. You will have to hustle to secure your first jobs. The competition for customers can be fierce in many parts of the country, and doing shoddy work can quickly erode your reputation. You might consider displaying your work at flea markets or home shows and expositions to get started. Practice your techniques on your own furniture and display only your best work.

Pricing your services can be tricky. Calculate the cost of materials, utilities and your time, then tack on 5 percent or so to cover the unexpected. Call around to competitors for their prices so you're sure you're in a reasonable ballpark. Don't skimp on materials – the end result will be a sub-par product. You'll have to forecast the time and materials you think each job will require so you can give customers estimates, then come in close to those estimates because you can't unexpectedly charge $100 more if you're wrong. Furniture refinishing is a solitary business and can become a little lonely, but it's also a good home business for a family team, like a husband and wife or parent and child.

Restoration of the backyard

Of course, this is a very unusual business idea, which can be implemented in any large city with an insufficient number of green areas for picnics. If you live in such a city and you have a cozy backyard, do not waste time until someone surpasses you! Customers can also choose something from additional equipment. For example, fully equipped grills and trampoline, ping-pong, kegs, slip-n-slide, a hill for riding, etc. these all will be available for an additional fee, of course.

Here are some ideas, which can make attract more clients, therefore it will let you expand your business.

Dining zone furniture. And the most diverse - wicker, forged, wooden, and sometimes just three options - this is eclectic. Colors - pastel or bright summer with floral prints.

Reservoirs. A rattling next to a flowing brook will present a particularly fabulous mood. If there is no rivulet nearby, it doesn't matter; you can install a fountain, build a small waterfall or even make an artificial pond.

Light. Garlands of lanterns will look just amazing summer evenings. Pendant candlesticks from the simplest cans look original; they can also be placed on garden furniture or ground if desired. Remember that solar garden lights are the safest and most economical option for backlighting at night.

Ornaments and décor. Old vintage furniture, bird cages, bird houses, bottles with herbs, a knitted grandmother's blanket and even a wooden door that no one needs anymore - all this can acquire a new life - and all this, of course, must be covered with flowers.

Vertical garden. Do not let the lack of space stop you from creating a beautiful garden. Vertical gardens of pocket type are popular for arrangement of a small area. The vertical design of the garden does not require much space. It can be made in different styles to suit your needs. Vertical gardening has the potential for use on the terrace, balcony and even the kitchen. The landscape of the yard with green vegetation will always look more fresh and natural.

Stone for paving tracks and gravel. It does not sound particularly glamorous, but a natural stone for paving plays an important role in creating an open space for your dreams. The paths from the house to the pool or the labyrinth of outdoor paths create order and separate the backyard into separate spaces: a dining area, a relaxation area, a barbecue area, a vertical one. Using natural stone in the production of landscape works, the private plot is transformed and becomes more natural and harmonious resembles the corner of wildlife. Take advantage of: paving slabs are hard enough to install furniture and interior items in the backyard.

Patio area. Turn a corner of space into a small entertainment center: a place for a fire, a barbecue grill, tables and chairs. Consider the layout plan carefully. You can pave a stone with a beautiful space that will allow you to enjoy the garden all year round. The correct design of the courtyard of the private house adds variety, style and functionality to the space, especially with so many wonderful ideas for the patio. See the photos and think about where to start.

A place for fire. One way to revive the backyard is to add a place to fire. The patio creates a collection point for friends and family. It also helps to light and warm the open space during cool nights! In addition, children can prepare marshmallows at the stake.

Terrace garden. When it comes to the garden, the limited space should not limit the originality and comfortable ideas of landscape design. Fill every nook of space with greenery. The use of frame structures will help increase the area for planting plants. Take a closer look at small garden structures, such as arbors, which can create a cozy place with a roof in a small space.

Use garden and wicker furniture. Garden furniture for decoration of the yard is made of thin branches of rattan, bamboo or willows, woven around a frame of a certain shape. Weaving requires a high level of skill, and this affects the price of the products. Wicker furniture for the patio does not fall apart after the first rain, but good care will increase the service life in dozens of times. It is necessary to protect garden furniture not only from the rain, but also from excessive sun, which can also cause harm. Excessive heat will make the furniture fragile and prone to damage. On sunny days, place wicker furniture from rattan in the shade as much as possible. Thus, you will spend noon in a pleasant shade, and for furniture provide more comfortable conditions, which will affect the service life.

These are just some of the ways how to decorate the yard with your own hands and make it more open. If you are not sure where to start, ask for advice from a friend of the gardener. It will help to select a landscape design and make an action plan. Try more ideas for building a yard. Be creative!

Repair and restoration of jewelry

Watch and jewelry repair shops handle a variety of repair services for their clients, including fixing new and antique watches, clocks, and jewelry items. Most people who request repair work on their watches or jewelry are bringing in antique or precious items with sentimental value, not to mention often high financial value. This increases your business risk due to the potential of damaging their precious heirlooms or having the items stolen from your shop. Therefore, you should get watch and jewelry repair business insurance in case something like this occurs.

As long as there's jewelry, there's a need for jewelry repair. Jewelry repair businesses provide a needed service. Skilled jewelry repair professionals can make a good income with the right resources.

Since there are many risks associated with a watch and jewelry repair business, there are also many insurance policies needed to cover each risk. The following are the most important types of watch and jewelry repair business insurance to consider purchasing for each of your probable risks.

General liability insurance includes personal injury, completed operations, and products liability. If a customer trips over box of items to be repaired and is consequently injured in your store, you'll likely have to pay their medical costs or be sued for damages. If you perform repair services on an antique necklace and cause more damage accidentally, that is also something you may be responsible for. General liability helps to cover these types of risks and more.

A common mistake for a small business owner is to launch your company without having written a business plan. The key benefit of writing a business plan is that it defines the game plan. If you don't have a business plan, your leadership will be handicapped, limiting your jewelry repair shop's ability to succeed long-term. Start by defining your business mission. The process of writing a mission statement doesn't have to be complicated. From there, you can begin to build on it with goals, budget estimates, marketing plans and other elements that are typically found in startup business plans.

How many potential customers will be within a fifteen-minute drive of your business? How many will be within an hour's drive of your business? It's important to run the numbers to understand how many customers might be interested in doing business with your local jewelry repair shop. Well in advance of opening a jewelry repair shop in your area, it's a smart move to see how you will fit in the competitive landscape. We've provided the link below to help you find competitors in your city. After following the link, enter your city, state and zip code to get a list of jewelry repair shops in your area. How tough is the competition in the market you are considering? If the competition is too tough, you may need to think about starting the business in a different area or even start a completely different business instead. After you've evaluated your local competitors, be sure to have a conversation with someone who is in the business. It's very unlikely that the local competition will talk to you. What's in it for them?

Fortunately, somebody who runs a jewelry repair shop in another town may be willing to share their entrepreneurial wisdom with you, as long as they don't view you as a competitive threat. Indeed, many experienced entrepreneurs enjoy offering advice to startup entrepreneurs. It can take a while to find an entrepreneur who is willing to talk, but its well worth the effort.

On a percentage basis, more entrepreneurs intend to enter jewelry repair shop ownership through a startup than through a business purchase. Yet jewelry repair shop startups aren't easy - many fail within the first year. There are a lot of factors that need to be considered in buying vs. starting a business. By buying a profitable jewelry repair shop, you'll shorten the amount of time it takes to achieve a return on your investment because you'll have the advantage of a proven operation and an existing customer base.

Purchasing a franchise doesn't mean you still can't fail but you do increase your odds of success when you buy a franchise. Before you get too far along in your plan to open a jewelry repair shop, you ought to check out whether buying a franchise could help you avoid common entrepreneurial mistakes. The link below gives you access to our franchise directory so you can see if there's a franchise opportunity for you. You might even find something that points you in a completely different direction.

Starting or growing a jewelry repair service takes work and planning. It starts with a business plan that shares your goals, research, marketing plans and developing customer relationships. Then build your business by networking through trade organizations. They also provide professional development. Taking these steps gets a repair business off the ground and keeps it growing.

Repair and restoration of swimming pools

If you are a lover of the great outdoors and have experience cleaning and maintaining swimming pools, a pool service company can be a great business to start from home. While some experience is necessary to do the job well, little equipment is required and startup costs can be less than $2,000. Some states require pool service companies to be certified by the public health department, so make sure your business is properly registered before you begin taking clients.

Create a business plan for your pool service business. Make a list of the services you will offer, the supplies you will need and how you will market yourself. Decide what you will specialize in, whether it be apartment complex swimming pools, hotel swimming pools or pools in affluent neighborhoods. Research other pool service companies in your area and determine how you can differentiate yourself by offering deeper knowledge, lower rates or other perks.

Name your company. Brainstorm a list of names that will appeal to your target audience. Set yourself apart from competitors by focusing your name on what makes your company original. For example, if your target market is affluent pool owners, choose a name that communicates class.

License your business. Go to your local city hall and request paperwork for registering your business. Don't start cleaning pools until you've secured an official license. Check with your public health department to see if your area requires special certification to legally clean pools.

Purchase necessary equipment. To start a swimming pool cleaning and repair business, you need to buy a pool skimmer, hoses, poles, pool-testing chemicals and pH test kits. Leaf rakes and scrub brushes are also good purchases. Lease or purchase a dependable vehicle with plenty of storage space for pool cleaning and repair equipment.

Gather pool service equipment and supplies. Shop locally and online to get the best prices on skimmers, water test kits, cleaning chemicals, leaf rakes and brushes for scrubbing. Consider buying chemicals in bulk for lower prices through online wholesalers. Secure a vehicle large enough to transport supplies to each work site.

Market your services. Create business cards to hand out as needed. Design fliers, brochures and door hangers that project an image of your company that will appeal to your target audience. If friendliness is your forte, make it known on your marketing materials; if professionalism or experience is your strong suit, incorporate it into your materials. List your services, including any areas of specialization as well as contact information. Hang door hangers in neighborhoods inhabited by your target market. Visit hotels, apartment complexes, health clubs and schools in person. Describe your services to them and drop off a business card and flier. Don't be afraid to contact them to follow up after a week or so. Keep in touch with potential clients so that even if they have a pool services company they work with, they will have you in mind if they need you.

Restoration of porcelain

Starting a porcelain enamel repair and refinishing business? This article discusses everything you should consider when opening a porcelain enamel repair and refinishing business.

A common mistake for a small business owner is to not create business plan for your startup porcelain enamel repair and refinishing business. The key benefit of writing a business plan is that it establishes both a framework and a roadmap for your business. The absence of an effective business plan inevitably results in impulsive leadership, choosing short-term opportunities at the expense of long-term benefits. The first step in creating a business plan is to develop a mission statement for your organization. From there, the other piece of the business plan puzzle will begin to fall in place.

Well in advance of opening a porcelain enamel repair and refinishing business in your area, it's essential to determine how strong the competition is. Try our link below to get a list of local competitors nearby. After clicking on the link, type in your city, state and zip code to get a list of porcelain enamel repair and refinishing businesses near you. Gain knowledge of how existing firms have positioned themselves in the marketplace, and then design your business in a way that sets you apart from the others.

If you want to open a porcelain enamel repair and refinishing business it's a smart move to have a conversation with someone who is in the business. It's very unlikely that the local competition will talk to you. What's in it for them?

Thankfully, an owner of a porcelain enamel repair and refinishing business in a different city may be willing to share their entrepreneurial wisdom with you, as long as they don't view you as a competitive threat. In that case, the business owner may be more than happy to discuss the industry with you. It can take a while to find an entrepreneur who is willing to talk, but its well worth the effort. How do you find a porcelain enamel repair and refinishing business owner in a different locale who can assist you? It's easy. Here's a link you can use to find a mentor outside of your area.

As a would-be porcelain enamel repair and refinishing business owner, the impulse to build a company from scratch is in your blood. But the harsh reality is that startup porcelain enamel repair and refinishing businesses experience a high failure rate compared to entrepreneurs who buy existing porcelain enamel repair and refinishing businesses.

There are a lot of factors that need to be considered in buying vs. starting a business. By buying a profitable porcelain enamel repair and refinishing business, you'll shorten the amount of time it takes to achieve a return on your investment because you'll have the advantage of a proven operation and an existing customer base.

The chances of becoming a successful entrepreneur immediately improve if you buy a franchise and benefit from the prior work of others and their lessons learned. If your goal is to start a porcelain enamel repair and refinishing business, you may want to check out whether franchising might make sense for you.

Repair and c (washing machines, refrigerators)

Everyone knows that getting a loan to buy new home appliances now is not too big a problem, but the technique is different, and sometimes it is cheaper to fix the old one than to acquire a new thing. For this reason, many people turn to service centers. According to expert data, this niche of the services market in percentage terms ranges from 20 to 35 units. The services of such a company can be used by both individuals and legal entities. And the call of the master can be made both in any district of the city, and beyond its limits - accordingly it will cost more.

The main strategy of an advertising campaign is to notify as many people as possible about the appearance on the market of repair services of a new company with high-quality and fast service and affordable prices. To attract potential customers, it is possible to hold a promo-promotion - for example, the first 50 clients will be able to receive a package of services at a discount. It will also be effective to conduct social surveys and fill out questionnaires for clients, which will help to eliminate possible mistakes at the initial stages.

Also, don't forget to sign a contract with a reliable call center and come up with a simple and easily memorable phone number of your workshop.

In the modern world, companies that undertake the responsibility of repairing household appliances - TV sets, refrigerators, microwave ovens, ovens and boilers, washing machines and dishwashers, as well as any other large- and small-sized household appliances, are divided into two types.

The first type (they are called mono brands) include such firms, which, in fact, are subsidiaries of a certain manufacturer and are engaged in repair and warranty maintenance of household appliances, created by this manufacturer (affiliated - that is, closely related to the main company and completely dependent on it, relatively independent, on the rights of equal cooperation).

The second type of machinery repair companies is multi brand firms. They undertake to repair any kind of equipment. This also includes such types of technical means as mobile phones and personal computers. Advantages of the second type are: high profitability (you do not need to pay for the brand name of the parent company), an expanded range of offered repair services - which means expanding the customer base to the limit.

Description of the services provided by the firm: repair of household appliances; TV, video and audio equipment; office equipment; In addition - repair of heating systems of a private house and apartment according to schemes and drawings.

Stages of fulfilling the sales order: obtaining equipment that requires repair, identifying the cause of the malfunction, searching for and selecting the necessary parts, eliminating the breakdown.

Remember that the better the repair and the faster the speed of service, the better reviews about you leave satisfied customers, and this is free advertising and a good way at the start to bypass competitors firms.

Features of the services provided: warranty maintenance of the repaired equipment within 3 months after the delivery to the client, delivery of equipment to the house and the workshop departure of the master for repairing the products of various manufacturing companies guarantee the safety of the equipment when it is impossible to carry out repairs.

This service is designed for the population with an average level of income - such people do not have the opportunity immediately after the breakdown of technology to purchase a new one. Proceeding from this, it is necessary to look for a room where there are a large number of such people. Promotion of the company in the market of services can be carried out by placing advertisements on the radio, in newspapers, when distributing or distributing leaflets. On the leased area there is a workshop with equipment and a customer service room.

CHAPTER 2. BECOME THE COORDINATOR OF EVENTS (BIRTHDAYS, WEDDINGS, CORPORATE PARTIES)

Do you throw great parties or meetings? Want to get paid doing it? Then you're ready for a job as an event coordinator. Event coordinators also known as event specialists, are in charge of every facet of meeting and events. This isn't just some wine and cheese affair with your buddies. Event coordinators plan everything from weddings to large expos and trade shows.

Event coordinators control an event from conception to clean up. They meet with clients to work out event details, plan with the client and their team, scout and book locations, food, entertainment, staff and cleanup. Event coordinators make sure the shrimp cocktail stays cold and the hired band stays hot. They create budgets and stick to them, as well as organize transportation, hire and wrangle keynote speakers or celebrities, hire A/V teams and equipment, and generally make sure the event runs smoothly, efficiently and handle any crisis that may come up.

Event coordinators, also known as event planners, work behind the scenes to organize every aspect of an event, from seating to speakers. If you choose this career path, it will be your job to see that everything comes off without a hitch. Read on to learn more. Schools offering Hospitality Management degrees can also be found in these popular choices.

Career Overview. As an event coordinator, you'll work with clients to find out what they expect of their occasion. After that, it's your job to coordinate the necessary people and materials to make sure your client's vision becomes a reality. To do so, you'll need a combination of business savvy and time management skills. You may also need to travel frequently to scout event locations, according to the U.S. Bureau of Labor Statistics (BLS, www.bls.gov). Because event coordinators must attend an event to see that all the details are in place, you may also have to put up with irregular work schedules and long days, as the job demands. Specialty areas within this field include meeting planners, corporate event planners, convention planners, and wedding planners.

Duties and Responsibilities. Also known as corporate event or convention planners, meeting planners scout, select, and negotiate contracts for appropriate event locations, such as conference rooms and convention halls. You may also need to register business clientele once they arrive or distribute surveys after the event to gauge its success, according to the BLS. Some events require planners or coordinators to create a marketing strategy that will attract potential attendees. Other tasks could include obtaining communications equipment, such as speakers or public announcement systems, and securing gift bags, VIP areas, or green rooms. Most venues and event planning services prefer candidates with a bachelor's degree related to planning or hotel service. Successful events coordinators have personal skills that include composure, communication, negotiation, problem-solving and organization.

CHAPTER 3. BECOME A TUTOR (MUSIC, DRAWING, LANGUAGES, SCHOOL SUBJECTS), IF YOU HAVE ANY SKILLS IN THIS

Tutoring is a wonderful way to earn money and hone teaching skills. As a tutor, you will have the advantage of working with individual students or small groups, which will allow you to customize your lessons to your students' pace, interests, and learning style. It doesn't matter whether you're tutoring adults or children: your students will respond to patience, attention, and personalized lessons.

Know your subject area. Aim to teach the subjects you know best. You are more likely to get hired to help someone with their essays and reading comprehension if you are an English Major, for instance. If you are hired to teach something you are not an expert in, get to know it.

If you are teaching something you have a strong personal knowledge of but have never learned in school, such as your own first language, take some time to study academic literature, lesson plans, and the rules your student must learn. If you are teaching your favorite thing, understand that your student may be struggling to understand it and may therefore not share your enthusiasm.

Make lesson plans. Plan each session ahead of time. Each lesson should include review of the previous lesson, introduction of a learning objective, and activities to help students practice applying what they have learned. Start with easier material, and make sure the student understands it before you move on. Let them do the parts they seem to understand without interfering. Move in to support them when they struggle with more difficult tasks. Guide students towards answers, but do not give them before the student has worked them out on their own. If a lesson doesn't go as planned, re-plan. Repeat tasks and take new angles on material that is harder for your student to learn.

Teach what you came to teach. Don't try to cover everything that comes up during class. Do not try to correct every mistake that your student makes. You can quickly overwhelm a student with information. Instead, take note of mistakes, but focus on your lesson goals. If you are teaching

English or a second language, never correct your student's grammar while they speak. Instead, model correct language usage.

Assess student comprehension. Ask your student to demonstrate what they have learned with you. Give quizzes, ask for verbal summaries, and check their work. You can also ask to be shown current test scores and completed class work to see if your student is demonstrating their knowledge outside of tutoring sessions. If a student does not seem to be absorbing the material, go back and re-explain from a different angle. Try starting further back, so your student can build up to the new material. If your student is getting teary, frustrated, or seems a blocked, switch activity or give them a break.

Build a personal relationship with your students. Students learn more effectively when they feel a friendly connection with their tutor. Build this rapport by greeting your student with a friendly smile, asking how they are doing, and truly listening to their answer. Take everything they say seriously, and respond thoughtfully. This doesn't mean that you should chat through your whole session. It just means that you should show interest in your student as a person, and let them see you as a person as well.

Personalize the lesson. Once you know your student better, you can tailor lessons to their interests and abilities. Start out by asking your student what they know about the subject. Listen for gaps—this is where you'll begin to fill in material they'll need to know.

Involve your student's interests in your lesson. For instance, if your student is really excited about a sports team, you can use that team's financial struggles as the basis for your math lesson. If you notice your student responds better to certain kinds of teaching, such as talking, reading, or hands-on practice, you can modify your lesson plans to favor this.

Come energetic and upbeat. Come in every day and make it very clear that you want to be there, you want to teach them the subject at hand, and that you know they can learn the material. Have confidence in yourself as a tutor, and have confidence in them that they will learn grow during the session. Make sure you thoroughly understand the material your student is learning even if it is not obviously interesting. If you pay attention to how something works, you will gain interest in it.

Get hired by a tutoring company. Tutoring companies can set you up with regular clients or with a small group. They will take a portion of the students' fees, but they may also pay wages and may be able to charge more per hour based on reputation. Some tutoring companies have a center with classrooms or cubicles, while others will send you on home visits. Consider test prep tutoring. If you don't mind covering highly standardized material, you can find regular work as a standardized test prep tutor. Many companies specialize in preparing students for tests like the SATs, ACT, TOEFL, and other tests. Look on job boards for tutoring company advertisements.

Advertise yourself independently. Make a profile on websites that showcase tutors. Make a flier advertising what you are willing to teach—be specific! If you say you can take any age and any subject, you'll sound unfocused. Say what ages you have experience with, what subjects you have tutored, and what metro area you are willing to work in. Include your contact information! You might say "Tutor: Elementary English-French-History-Creative Writing. I have three years of experience as a TA and tutor for 3-5th graders. I am up to date on student learning standards in this range. I'm also great at making learning fun." Contact local schools to offer tutoring services. If you're in school, get in touch with your campus Writing Center or Learning Lab and ask about tutoring opportunities. Most schools hire student tutors to work with their peers. Contact friends you know who teachers are or who know people who might be potential clients of yours.

Consider tutoring online. Many students are looking for tutoring in subjects that are less available where they live. This includes students abroad, students in rural areas, homeschooled students, and students who can't easily leave the house. Look on job boards or google "online tutoring" to find companies that will let you advertise your services.

Figure out how much to charge. Tutors in different areas charge wildly different rates. Ask other tutors who do more or less what you want to do what they charge. Ask multiple people to get a clear sense. Check places where tutors in your area advertise as well. You may charge more for extra experience or expertise in a subject. For instance, if you graduated college with a degree in computer science, you should charge more than a self-taught high school student. You don't necessarily have to advertise your rate. You can wait for your clients to make an offer, but you should have a rate in your head that you won't go below.

Communicate with parents and teachers. If you have been hired by a family, your student's parents likely have specific learning goals for their children. They may be able to communicate with you what the concepts are that their child has been struggling with. If you are working for a school, speak with the subject or classroom teacher and get informed on what the classroom is working on, what the student is struggling with, and things the teacher things your student might respond to. Stay in communication with the parents and teacher of your student; so that you call update one another on milestones and roadblocks. If you are working for elementary and secondary students, keep up with the learning standards of their grade. You can usually find out what the

Learning Standards are for each grade on the school district website.

Use incentives. Some students will be motivated to do well just by a desire to please their parents, their teacher, you, or themselves. Others will need some encouragement. Praise good work to encourage them, and give a little praise for good effort as well. Smaller students respond well to stickers that signify the completion of a lesson or a task. Older students might enjoy greater responsibility or a change of routine. You might tutor them outside for one session if they achieve a certain improvement in their grade, for instance. Some students will be incentivized if you let them set the learning goals for each lesson with you. Some students want you to be in control of their learning, but will feel rewarded if you explain what they have learned and how that has affected what you are going to teach them next.

Give your students opportunities to move. Children, especially small children, need to move. Transition activities every 15-20 minutes, and provide movement breaks and a few minutes for free play every 45 minutes or when needed. If you only tutor your student for half an hour or so, you can just give them breaks as needed. If they need to move but your time is limited, try switching locations or give your students a short but intense physical movement break. Offer regular opportunities for dancing, jumping on a trampoline, running around the yard, or doing some quick pushups. Let the student cue you when they need to move.

They may ask to get a glass of water, to go to the bathroom, or to get something to show you from their room. Watch for squirming, kicking, head-in-hands—this could mean a student has physical energy that is distracting them. Some students may prefer to work standing up or sitting on the floor.

Get experience with kids. One way you can gain experience is by volunteering as a tutor. Contact local schools or family friends and volunteer to take on short-term tutoring projects. Get in touch with your local library-they may have a volunteer program for reading buddies or some other low-key tutoring experience. Set up a language exchange with someone who speaks a language you are learning. You can take turns tutoring one another.

CHAPTER 4. TAKE UP FREELANCING (DESIGN, PHOTOGRAPHER, TRANSLATION OF TEXTS, COPYWRITING, DEVELOPING OF WEBSITES)

While it's possible to survive and even succeed as a freelance graphic designer without formal education, it is very difficult to do so. Besides, being the very best designer you can be is the name of the game, so why not learn as much as possible?

Go to school. While it is possible to survive and even succeed as a freelance graphic designer without formal education, it is very difficult to do so. Besides, being the very best designer you can be is the name of the game, so why not learn as much as possible? You can choose either a short term certificate program or a long term degree program to get your design education. Decide based on your budget and the amount of time you have.

Perfect your software knowledge. As a graphic designer, you want to have a working knowledge of the primary programs in the field. These include Adobe Photoshop, Adobe Illustrator, InDesign, and many others. However, you probably have (or will have) a favorite program that you feel most comfortable with. Use it, and practice with it, as much as you can.

Keep an eye on pop culture. Every good graphic designer is also a student for life. Watch for signs of trends and breakthroughs in the world of graphic design. Look at magazines and newspapers regularly to see what types of designs are popular. Read about current trends online. Never let yourself become out of touch.

Find your niche. As a freelance graphic designer, you are going to be facing a lot of competition for work, including from the big firms. You have to determine what makes you stand out; what will make customers come to you. Whether it is lower price, better customer service, faster turnaround time, or whatever, figure it out and get ready to flaunt it.

Market yourself. Now you are ready to advertise your services. You can use your own design talents to help out in this area, by designing your own brochures and posters. Get in the habit of handing out business cards to everyone you meet. Join clubs and groups in your area and get to know people. Market with friends and associates. Do everything you can to get your name out there and let people know that you are a talented graphic designer available for hire.

Get to work. If you have talent and work hard, you will have business in no time. Make sure you always give your clients more than they are paying for. Do everything they ask of you and more. And always provide exceptional customer service. If they are not happy with something, redo it for them at no charge.

When photography is your passion, deciding to become a freelance photographer may seem like an easy decision. Learning how to run a successful photo business, though, is a little more complicated. That's because your success doesn't just rest on your photography skills; you have to be able to carry all the administrative duties as well.

Choose a specialty. When you're a professional photographer, you can specialize in different types of photography, such as news, weddings and other special events, or portraits. However, if you plan to freelance, it's even more important to focus your business because you'll need to know what type of equipment and accessories you'll need and how to market your business. You don't have to necessarily limit yourself to one specialty, though, because you'll often attract more business if you offer more services. For example, you might advertise yourself as an event and portrait photographer. Those two specialties go well together because a couple who hired you to shoot their wedding and liked their photos may remember you when it comes time to have their children's portraits taken.

Event photography typically means taking photos at weddings, parties, graduations, and other special events. If you specialize in portrait photography, you'll be taking photos of individuals, which often means families, children, and even pets. Commercial and product photography usually involves taking photos of products, properties, and other items to help a business market themselves. Stock photography refers to photos that are taken for the sole purpose of being sold. You can sell your photos through a stock photo agency, where individuals and businesses that need a photo of a certain object or situation can purchase them. News photographers take pictures of noteworthy events and people. While it can be an exciting job, it's extremely difficult to break into the field as freelancer if you don't have previous experience.

Get a business license. Like any business, a freelance photography business needs some type of permit or license to operate in your city, county, or state. In most cases, you need a general business license. However, if you are running your business out of your home, you may also need a Home Occupancy Permit. Don't start taking any photos before you have the necessary license.

Consider taxes. As a freelancer, it will be your responsibility to pay both federal and state taxes because they won't be automatically taken out of your earnings as they would be by an employer. Because it can be somewhat confusing, it's usually a good idea to consult an accountant, whose knowledge and expertise can often help save you money. Try to find an accountant who specializes in small businesses, so you can trust that they're up to date on all the tax codes and benefits that will affect you. You can also ask your accountant for advice on what type of structure your business should take. Most photography businesses are usually sole proprietorships, meaning they're owned by a single person who receives all of the profits.

Set fees. Before you can start lining up clients, you need to know how much you plan to charge for your services. When it comes to creating a fee schedule, you should factor in expenses such as equipment, taxes, and operation fees. However, you should also consider the time that goes into each project, including transportation time, so you can ensure that you're making enough money to survive. There are various types of software, such as foto Quote and Blink Bid that help you estimate the costs involved in photography projects and create invoices for your customers.

CHAPTER 5. BECOME AN INTERNET MARKETER (INSTAGRAM, GOOGLE ADWORDS, FACEBOOK). IT'S NOT SO DIFFICULT TO LEARN

Internet marketing is the job of creating a convincing message that attracts customers to an online product. Successful online marketers come from a variety of backgrounds, including business, graphic design, writing and IT fields. You can find resources on the Internet. Trying on a small initial project and add the results to your personal work portfolio. Use the portfolio to interview for jobs in the field, or to find work as a freelancer.

Decide if marketing is a career fit for you. Consider taking a personality test, which will reveal your preferences. A test similar to the popular Myers-Briggs test can be found at 16personalities, and there are many others. This test will reveal your work preferences. See how of your preferences match the skills needed to be an Internet marketer. Marketing is the process of getting attention and generating interest for a product or service. Marketers spend a lot of time communicating with people about their needs and preferences. A marketer thinks about how they can meet those customer needs. Professionals in marketing come from a wide variety of backgrounds. Many marketers earn a college degree in business or marketing. However, the marketing field also requires graphic artists, writers and programmers. Marketing requires creativity. That creativity can come in many forms. Graphic designers put together visual presentations to attract customers. Writers create content that is designed to engage the reader and keep them interested. A programmer writes code to create a web page that is easy to navigate. Regardless of your marketing role, you need to think creatively.

Learn about the components of the Internet marketing profession. Internet marketing requires a variety of tasks. To decide which areas are a good fit for you, find resources to learn about each task. Fortunately, there many free resources you can access. A majority of Internet use now takes place on mobile devices. It's critical for a marketer to understand how a website looks on mobile. Users want a site that is simple and easy to navigate on mobile. Google has put an increased focus on good content. If you consistently post useful content, your site will move up in Google search results. Knowledge about content marketing is become more important for Internet marketers. Your degree program will provide a base of marketing knowledge. Business, graphic design and technology degrees all include marketing as part of the curriculum. Your college courses provide a good starting point. Read blogs and articles and educate yourself about the industry. Search Engine Land and Marketing Land are two excellent websites for Internet marketing. You can subscribe to these sites to stay on top of the industry. You can also perform a web search to find other current topics on Internet marketing. You can find a You Tube video that explains just about any task you perform as an Internet marketer. Keep a list with the You Tube links that you find the most useful. You can refer back to those videos when you need a refresher.

Build your skills through education and your portfolio of work. Once you have an overview of the profession, you can decide on the right type of college degree for your marketing career. You can also start to build a portfolio of work from school and internships. Many marketers get a marketing degree through their school's business department. Other successful Internet marketers have degrees in communications, graphic design or IT. Because this field requires several different types of skills, you can enter the field with each of these degrees. It's important to build an online portfolio that displays your work as an Internet marketer. Most people have a website with links to work they have performed. When a potential client is interested in you, they can review your website to find out what you've done in the field. Your portfolio can have still photos of web pages you have built for clients. You can also provide links to client pages and testimonials from your customers. Make sure that you have a complete and current LinkedIn profile. LinkedIn may be the first place a potential employer visits to find out more about you. Fill out your LinkedIn profile completely and connect with people you know. Start to think about taking on projects as a freelancer. You can find projects on large employment sites like Monster.com. If you simply search the web using "freelance Internet marketing jobs", you'll find job boards that are updated weekly. Craigslist is also a great source for freelance work.

Take on a small project to build your skills. Whether you plan on interviewing for a marketing job, or decide to become a freelancer, you need some experience. Consider taking on a small project to apply your marketing knowledge. You may handle all of the components of an Internet marketing project, or only a portion of the work. In many cases, freelancer marketers collaborate with other professionals. If you're just starting out, you may complete a portion of an Internet marketing project. There are many entities that need Internet marketing, but only budget a small amount for the work. If you're willing to volunteer or offer a discounted rate, you can find projects. Non-profit entities and political campaigns need marketing help, but don't have much money budgeted for the work. These types of organization may present an opportunity for you. Ask the company if you can include the work in your professional portfolio. You need to build a portfolio of work to interview for jobs or to do find freelance work. Say, for example, that you design the layout for a website. You can include still photos and a link to the site you created in your portfolio. Most marketing professionals have a personal website to display their work and promote their skills.

Select the Internet marketing skills you will use in your work. Whether you're interviewing for a job or looking for freelance work, you need to decide what skills you will offer. Consider the components of an Internet marketing campaign and decide which tasks you will perform. Decide on a writing or communication focus for your work. Content marketing is becoming a critical way to market online. If a website can post interesting blogs and articles, they can drive traffic and attract business. You may decide to specialize in writing great content. You can also apply your writing skills to text on a web page and to sales materials.

Some marketers focus on the advertising component of Internet marketing. You can focus on the keywords and phrases that entice people to click on an add You can also help clients with search engine optimization (SEO). SEO is the process of changing a website's content to increase the site's ranking in a search result. These marketers also help clients build links between pages and websites.

If you have a programming emphasis, you can write code to make a website's navigation simply and easy to use. Programmers use code to improve the functionality of websites. You may decide to learn all of these roles and manage the entire Internet marketing process. This approach requires management skills, so you have the ability to keep an Internet marketing campaign on track.

Focus on social media marketing. Consumers spend an increasing amount of time on social media sites, such as Twitter and Facebook. You can help your clients reach their target audience through social media marketing. Make sure that you understand all of the potential marketing opportunities on LinkedIn. All of your customer's key employees should have complete profiles on LinkedIn. Those managers should also post articles and blog links to the site frequently. People use LinkedIn to network, find business and also look for jobs. Use your marketing knowledge to ensure that your clients have a presence on LinkedIn.

Set up an attractive Twitter page for your clients. Post to the firm's Twitter account frequently, using links to blogs and articles. Make sure that your client understands how to use hash tags to reference topics. You can help clients create an effective Facebook page. Facebook allows you to post more text, pictures and graphics that Twitter. As your customers post on social media, you need to ensure that prospects and customers can easily click through to the company website. Make sure that all the social media sites make it easy for customers to get to the firm's website.

Look for a job in the field. Use all of your available resources to find an Internet marketing job that interests you. Access your school's placement office and your personal network to find job postings. If you're earning a college degree, ask your college placement office for help. They can tell you the types of jobs graduates are finding in your particular field. The placement office may have potential employers visit your campus.

Contact people in your personal network and find out about their business contacts. Look for individuals who work in the marketing field. Your network can refer to you into companies that may be interviewing for marketers. You can also find a mentor to help you consider jobs in the marketing field.

Perform a search for Internet marketing jobs on the web. You can search for jobs in the specific marketing fields you prefer. In today's job market, employers increasingly use the Internet to find qualified candidates. While you will face a large number of other job candidates, searching for jobs on the web can pay off.

Prepare for your interview. Your interview may be for a full-time job or for work with a new freelance client. In both cases, you need to prepare for your interview. Learn everything you can about the firm and its marketing needs. If possible, find someone in your network that knows about the firm. Perform Internet research about the company.

Put together an effective portfolio of your work. In most cases, your portfolio will be on your personal website. Send the interviewer a link to your personal website before the meeting. Be prepared to talk about your prior work.

Explain how your marketing skills can solve problems for your client. Read the company's job requirements carefully. Connect your skill set to the outcomes the employer wants. For example, you may explain how you can put together great content to build website traffic. Explain how the additional traffic can increase sales and profits.

CHAPTER 6. BECOME A YOUTUBE BLOGGER IN AN AREA THAT YOU KNOW WELL (WHERE YOU ARE A PROFESSIONAL)

It's a lot of fun to blog, but it can get old fast if no one is visiting! Getting your blog to the top of the search engines for your main key phrases should be your goal to make this traffic happen. Keep in mind that it will take time, but it's very possible. Being a vlogger - or video blogger - seems really cool, but gaining and audience is harder than it sounds. Preparing before becoming a vlogger can really help you along your path to becoming a successful vlogger.

Think of a topic to make vlogs about. It can be anything, as long as it's not boring, insulting, or illegal. Take other video bloggers as an inspiration, such as Casey Neistat, Katersoneseven, Charlieissocoollike, Nerimon, Frezned, Italktosnakes, or Vlogbrothers. But you have to be unique and true to yourself. Don't be a copycat - don't do what everyone else does.

Be yourself. When you are being yourself in your videos, you begin to become comfortable with yourself. The danger of not being yourself is destroying trust with your subscribers. If you try to be someone else in your videos, which means you'll be acting in front of the camera every day. That can become tiring and un-fun.

Get a YouTube account, and give your channel an attractive name. Make your channel interesting. Make sure you think over your username, though, because it's nearly impossible to make it big with a jumbled, unreadable username with a bunch of numbers!

Consider your audience. Are you reaching out to the younger people? Older people? What are you going to be vlogging about? Consider these questions before making your way onto YouTube.

Make about ten or more really good videos. They really have to be good, and interesting. Post one or two daily for a little while, and then go daily or every other day after that. Really try not to skip two days, because what you give your viewers becomes their standard.

Don't hide emotions in your videos. Vlogging is like your diary. You show your emotions and tell your audience how you feel. Don't get on camera and act happy when you know you are feeling bad. Tell your viewers how you're feeling.

Post one of those videos to a related, well-known video as a video response. You will get at least a fifth of the views of the original video! Awesomeness TV on YouTube allows you to post video responses to their how to be a YouTube star series.

Edit your videos! This means the difference of viewers scrolling past you and clicking on your videos. Look at tutorials on using the software you have. Windows has Windows Movie Maker preinstalled, and all Apple products have iMovie available. Android has Movie Maker preinstalled.

Surround yourself with positive people. Allow people into your life only if they are there to motivate you, not bring you down. When people are always criticizing you, sometimes that can affect your day and potentially ruin your mood. Talk things through with your family. See if they want to be in your vlogs. Ask them questions and see if they are.

Keep being active - nobody is going be interested if you don't post any videos for years also sometimes put your tittle of your video in CAPITALS to get people more interested. If possible, try to set a specified day that you will upload videos.

For a vlogger, at least three or four times a week. If this is too much, try to do one per week.

Consider the relationship you're in. Sometimes, putting your life on the internet may not always be suitable for your partner. Talk it through with your partner and see if it's okay! There are dangers of vlogging your life on YouTube when you are in a relationship, because viewers are prone to criticizing it whether or not they know it. It will sometimes make you doubt your relationship.

Another danger is "not knowing." Sometimes, having a relationship with a person while on camera can become confusing. You will end up trying to figure out if you really love that person, or if your love for that person is only for the camera. Consider your relationship before making the step to become a vlogger.

Once you have a good reputation in the YouTube community, try to become a YouTube partner. You will need to have at least a few thousand views to do so. YouTube gives you money for allowing ads to be displayed on your videos, and that's how great vloggers earn money with their videos! Your videos will appear often in search results as well.

When you first start your vlogs, don't expect to gain one million subscribers in one day. Technically, when you first get on YouTube, you're probably like, "Oh my gosh, I'm going to be famous now!" This isn't really true. It takes years to gain that many subscribers, and once you realize that you don't have as many subscribers as you intended, you get frustrated easily.

Set realistic goals for yourself. Maybe in one video, try to get just five views on that video. Then on the next video, try to get ten views. Improve yourself and gradually build your views and subscribers.

Become a "yes man." If your subscribers want you to do something, try to do it! It will build their trust in you. Know when to say no. Some things that people will want you to do may not be healthy or good for you. Nicely tell your viewers in one of your vlogs how you feel about it. Remember! Your viewers are your family, so you must talk it through with them.

Don't listen to the haters. Sure, you might notice a few dislikes here and there, but you should focus on what brings you joy. You should be too focused on making a difference than the negativity that is thrown at you.

CHAPTER 7. OPEN THE TRUCK WITH FOOD AND DRINKS (COFEE). WITH THE SUBSEQUENT GROWTH OF A NUMBER OF TRUCK

Food trucks are one of the hottest trends in the culinary industry with a significant growth rate. If you like cooking and serving people, you might be considering opening up your own food truck, which can be less expensive than starting a restaurant. But you may be unsurprising of how to start your food truck. By getting yourself set up and building your business, you can start a food truck!

Talk to food truck owners. Before you take concrete steps to start your food truck, consider talking to other food truck owners. They can answer questions you have and may help offer you practical advice for setting up your business. Ask questions about how she set up her food truck. See if she experienced any setbacks that could have been prevented with preparation or can suggest ways to cut startup and operations costs.

Consider your goals and lifestyle. Think about how owning a food truck can fit into your life. Factors such as your career and financial goals, time, location, and possible can help guide your decision and shape your truck as you get set up. Ask yourself some of the following questions: What are the physical demands? Operating a food truck will probably require that you spend long hours standing on your feet. Are there emotional demands? Running a successful business can put a lot of emotional stress on you between trying to succeed and make money as well as the time it may take away from loved ones. Does the business fit your personality?

Owning a food truck means you rely on the public to support your business. Customer service is going to be a big part of your job and if you enjoy working with and interacting with others, this could be a great choice for you.

Come up with a preliminary concept. Design a basic concept to guide you as you get the food truck set up. Thinking about the food you want to serve and your image can help you more easily formulate you business plan. Ask around to find out which food trucks do the most business in order to get an idea of the types of food that potential patrons may find appealing. Speculate on what types of food trucks may do well even though they do not currently exist within your municipality. For instance, if cupcake trucks do well in your area but no one has tried other dessert trucks, you could experiment with a specialty-dessert truck. Consider having a taste test before finalizing your concept. Anonymous surveys and taste tests can help determine whether or not there is any interest in your truck.

Establish your legal business entity. Set up a legal entity to give your food truck business some legitimacy. Establishing a legal entity, which includes your business plans, can persuade potential investors and clients that your food truck is a serious business.

Write business plans. Draft and finalize both a short- and long term business plan that can guide your business. Not only is this is important to help develop your business and accommodate for contingencies like a lawsuit, but it can also help you secure financing to buy permits, insurance, and supplies. Write out the goals and objectives for your truck, what financing you have and need, any marketing strategies, and how you will implement your business plan.

Apply for licenses, permits and certificates. Mobile restaurants need different types of permits and licenses for their trucks and cooking facilities than regular restaurants. Ask local authorities about what you need. You can also consult with other food truck owners to ensure you obtain the correct licenses and certificates.

Apply for insurance. Just as a regular vehicle, your food truck—and business- need insurance. This can protect your assets and from any liability if your truck hits someone. Be aware that cost of insurance can vary depending on the company that insures you, but it should not be much higher than regular vehicle insurance. Let the underwriter know about any risks your food truck might present. For instance, if you plan to store propane tanks on the truck, your insurance underwriter can incorporate this into your policy.

Stock your truck with kitchen equipment. If you plan on preparing food in your truck, you will need storage and cooking appliances. Stock the unit with anything you need immediately and add supplies as they become necessary. Get basic storage supplies including a refrigerator, freezer, and cupboards for ingredients and utensils. Buy basic preparation and cooking supplies such as an oven, fryer, countertops, cutting boards, and utensils like plates and silverware. Consider renting commercial kitchen space if you want to prepare the food off-site. If you can find affordable kitchen to rent and a cheap, basic truck, this might be more cost-effective.

Contract food vendors. You'll need to work with vendors to supply the food or ingredients for your dishes. Making contracts with specific vendors can not only help cut costs but may also get you business by word of mouth.

Call multiple vendors and discuss your food truck. Ask the vendor questions about quality and pricing. Check the vendor's references. Find out their current customers and if those restaurants or food trucks are satisfied with the vendor's performance. Make sure that the quality of the product is good, as well as the quality of the service. Verify that any meat, dairy, or perishable food items are shipped in a timely and sanitary manner. Ask to see health inspection reports and permits.

Limit your vendors. Keeping track of a large quantity of invoices can bog down your business. Consider sticking with a couple of key vendors for your needs.

Buy in bulk from non-contract sources. If you prefer to buy supplies yourself instead of dealing with food vendors, consider buying in bulk from catalogs and warehouses. Be aware that you will need to provide proof that the vendor meets health inspection standards for its products.

Find a place to park your truck. Food trucks are large and require a space to park when they are not operating. Some cities will require you to rent space at a city-owned truck lot, while others let you to rent your own depot or commissary space as long as it is approved by health inspectors. Check with your local authorities about specific regulations and procedures for parking your truck. Check that your depot or commissary offers power to store the truck overnight, fresh water, and a place to fill up your propane.

Work with a mentor. Ask an experienced businessperson who understands small businesses or the restaurant industry to serve as a mentor for your business. She can help you grow and offer advice during difficult times or situations.

Price your items fairly. Set up prices structure for your food. Remember that you'll need to charge enough to cover operational costs and make a profit. Figure out range of prices and then set a final price once you've had a chance to research what other trucks charge for similar dishes and calculated your own costs. Gauge your prices are commensurate with similar trucks in your local area.

Listen to customer demands. Pay close attention to your customers' suggestions and requests. This can help you retain, and gain, customers. Be flexible without changing your entire concept. For example, if you sell gourmet cupcakes but you find customers turning away because you do not have traditional flavors, compromise by having a selection of traditional and gourmet flavors. Ask customers what they like and why they like it. Chatting with your customers can bring a lot to your business. Hang up a suggestion box on the side of the truck and check it daily.

Stay on top of industry trends. Because food trucks are increasingly popular, staying on top of industry trends is important to keeping your business fresh and attracting customers. Read trade publications, network with food truck owners, and eat at other food trucks to keep yourself informed.

CHAPTER 8. OPEN A VISITING BUSINESS IN THE FIELD OF BEAUTY (MANICURE, HAIRSTYLES, PEDICURE, EYEBROWS)

Find how much you need and create a budget. Get a business license and pass any health inspections. Hire qualified and trained people.

Figure out how much money you need. Starting a business can cost a lot of money, and most entrepreneurs don't turn a profit for the first year or two. Here's what to consider: Can you still support yourself while your business gets up and running? Calculate how much money you need for monthly expenses, how much of a cushion you have in savings, and how much you absolutely must make each month to stay afloat.

Come up with an operating budget. Calculate how much money you'll need to run your business every month. Include rent, licensing, training, payroll, supplies and an emergency fund. Figure out how much you'll charge for services. Once you have an operating budget, you'll know how much money you need to break even each month. To make a profit, though, you'll need to do more than break even. Estimate how many services (such as haircuts, colors, manicures, etc.) you might perform in a week and figure out how much they need to cost in order for you to make money. Keep in mind that though you need to charge enough to be profitable, you can't charge too much — or you'll drive away customers. Try to set a price point that is both fair for your clients and prosperous for you. Get an idea of what other salons charge. Browse comparable salons in your area, and take note of what they charge. Your prices should probably be in a similar range.

Offer a wide range of services. This could give you a distinct advantage over those who offer only one or two types of services. Many clients prefer to have their hair, nails and face done in one place, instead of going to three different places. While you can specialize in one main area (for example hair), giving your clients the convenience of a one-stop beauty shop can set your business apart from your competitors.

Keep your clients satisfied. It is important that your business create and maintain the desirable reputation as a quality hair and salon operation, so that your clients keep returning for maintenance. Try to give them the best possible experience each time, and go out of your way to make them feel valued.

CHAPTER 9. WALK WITH DOGS, OR TAKE THEM TO YOURSELF FOR OVEREXPOSURE (OR ANY OTHER ANIMALS)

Do you dream of being a pet sitter/dog walker? If the answer is 'yes', then keep reading! This article will show you how to do it easily.

First of all, think of a name for your pet sitting/dog walking business. Decide how much you're going to charge for what service. Will you charge for how long you walk/look after the dog? Will you charge more if the dog is badly behaved and you have to control it more? Think about these things. If you just want to walk/look after dogs for fun, you can offer your services for free!

Put yourself out there to the world. Nobody is going to know about you if you don't advertise. You need to make posters advertising your dog walking service. Your poster **should have the following on it:** the name of your dog walking/pet sitting business; the services you provide; when you're available (weekdays, weekends, after school?); how much you charge; means of contacting you (phone number and/or email address); a little bit about you (are you a student? Do you have previous pet ownership experiences?).

Once you've made up your posters, put them around in as many places as possible. Tape them to streetlamps; post them at community centers, schools, and supermarket bulletin boards. If you don't attract the attention of other people, your business will never get off the ground.

Once you get your first customer, **be friendly** to them and do a good job with their pets. Show them that you're a trustworthy person. People love their dogs, and if you do a good job of taking care of them, your customers will talk to their friends and recommend you to them. Word will get around and will earn you even more customers. All you have to do is be trustworthy, polite, and professional.

After doing all of these steps, your pet sitting/dog walking business should really get off of the ground! You may have to be patient, but the results will eventually come, and you might end up making a fair bit of money! Good luck!

CHAPTER 10. BECOME A NURSE FOR CHILDREN (NANNY, BABYSITTER)

Having to watch children that are not your own can be a difficult task, but taking time to do research on that family is exciting. Knowing who you is about to watch is a big factor in babysitting.

Match your age to the task. Check the ages of the child or children needing babysitting. Depending on your age, this impacts the age of the kids you can be responsible for. If you're around this age (15 or younger) it's best to babysit an older kid about 10 years old and upward, children that can do most things for themselves. And it's best around this age to make sure the child can entertain themselves, as they may not be keen to interact with you. If you're 16 or older, you should be able to babysit younger children. You must be comfortable handling small children. You should have more responsibility at this age. No matter what the age of the child, don't leave any child alone. You are there to take care of them, no matter what.

Ask questions. When you're ready to go in the babysitting business, don't be afraid to ask questions about the child you will be caring for; always be prepared.

Bring with you pen and paper for emergency information, important phone numbers and directions to the house as soon as you arrive. Bring an emergency checklist just in case the parents don't have one. Show the parents these things, as it helps to reassure them.

Let the parents know that you do believe in discipline and you won't let a child run over you. Explain that you will be strict about bedtime and not viewing unacceptable websites, and so one.

Gather things you might do with the kids. Include things that are within the child's interests. Consider bringing a small prize for each child at the end if they're good, such as a sticker sheet or small toy). A sample list could be: crayons and coloring pages, a movie, board games, a cookie recipe, etc.

Be aware that the children might do things that might be frightening to you sometimes, such as throwing a tantrum, tossing toys or yelling at you. Just act in much the same way that you would if they were your own sisters and brothers and do your best to calm them down. Give a timeout if they're really misbehaving, or call the parents for advice.

Walk through the house and do safeties check. Close the doors to rooms you don't want the children in. Look for hazards such as matches, hanging electrical cords, medications or other things children can get hurt with or get into trouble with. Check with the parents or guardians for any last minute phone numbers and contact details.

Spend time getting to know the children better. Every child acts a certain way when parents aren't around.

Interact. Instead of laying back on the couch watching some TV, play with the kids. It's more fun if the babysitter actually plays "House" or "Dolls" or whatever the game may be. If you have a smart phone, download a couple of educational apps and interact that way. The parents will appreciate it later!

Smile. Be positive, patient, and never yell. If the kids are acting up, warn them that they won't get a special prize at the end of the day. If you're happy, the kids most likely will be, too.

Play outdoors if there is daylight. Take the kids out to play. They can play tag and games like that. Try to play with them, too. The kids can play games like basketball and soccer with you. Make sure the kids wear sun block approved by the parents. If you have permission from the parents, maybe take the kids out for a walk with the dog or take them out to ride their bike at the park.

Prepare food. Check the cabinets and cook a snack or meal, as required. Make easy food, such as chicken nuggets or mac and cheese. Make sure to include veggies with the meal. Green beans or corn, for example. Give the kids a small snack if babysitting throughout the day, such as fruit or fruit chews. For dinner, give the kids something the parents have planned or asked you to prepare. For dessert, give them something like ice cream.

Allow the kids to do something fun before bedtime. You can bring a craft set you bought like a jewelry maker, games, a create your own car set, or a toy airplane set. You can bring coloring books and paper and even paints. Maybe even let them explore the web with their parents permission and your supervision.

Get the kids to bed on time, as requested by the parents. Just read them a favorite story and shut out the lights. Keep ears out for any crying, calling out or anything else the kids are doing besides sleeping. They remain your responsibility until the parents walk back in through the door.

CHAPTER 11. LEASE YOOUR FREE PROPERTY FOR RENT

The vacation rental industry has changed rapidly in the last several years, and it's now easier than ever to rent out your home or condo on a long or short-term basis. Whether you'd like to permanently convert your home into a vacation rental, or just rent out your apartment for a few weeks while you're on vacation, there are people out there who want to rent it, and websites and services that will help make it happen. Do keep in mind that renting out your home can be a major undertaking, so it is important to know what you are getting into, and to prepare accordingly. With a little bit of planning and hard work, you can put your home to work for you, and meet a lot of new and interesting people in the process.

Determine whether or not your property would make a suitable vacation rental. Before you invest a lot of time and money getting ready to rent, you should first ensure that your home is rentable. Is it in a desirable location? Is it near popular attractions in your town? Does the home have any amenities or unique features that would make it particularly desirable?

If there are other vacation rentals in your neighborhood, that is an excellent sign that your home is rentable. Search online for highly-rated listings in your area. Are there many listings in your area? Does your home offer similar amenities? Are you willing to add or upgrade amenities to make the home a desirable rental?

Make sure you can legally rent out your home or condo. There are numerous levels of laws and restrictions that might regulate rental homes in your area. Do your research now to avoid paying expensive fines in the future.

Decide if you want to rent seasonally, year-round, or as a short-term vacation swap. You may just want to rent your home out for a few weeks while you are on vacation, or turn it into a permanent rental property. Think carefully about what you want to do, so that you can prepare accordingly. Some locations have very different regulations on short-term and long-term rental properties. These vary widely from place to place, so learn about the laws in your area before you commit to a rental plan.

Decide if you want to rent your whole home, or only a room or two. If you are thinking about renting out only a portion of your home, think carefully about what that will entail to determine if you are up for the challenge.

Apply for a rental permit. Permits are not necessary in all areas, especially for short-term rentals, but many cities are responding to the growth of new rental trends by creating new forms of regulation. If a permit is required in your area, give yourself plenty of time to get through the application process before your first guests arrive.

Screen your guests carefully. Inviting strangers into your rental home can be a nerve-wracking, risky process. Create a protocol for screening new guests that will help alleviate some of your fears.

CHAPTER 12. COOK SWEETS AT HOME. SELL VIA THE INTERNET

Home-based businesses allow entrepreneurs to make a living while saving on commuting costs and childcare. Selling products from home can be profitable if there is high demand for the product. Some salespeople create homemade goods, while others re-sell used or wholesale items. The right product, combined with efficient organization and time management skills, can help you be successful as you sell products from home.

Brainstorm what type of products you have knowledge of and could succeed in selling from home. What do you enjoy doing? Most people enjoy working on projects where .they feel skilled in. What's yours?

If you are skilled in crafting, sewing or cooking you may decide to make and sell home décor, accessories, jewelry or edible items. If you have an eye for bargains you may be interested in buying and re-selling antiques or other items. If you enjoy working with a network of business owners and socially interacting with your customers, you may consider becoming a consultant for an existing home-based direct sales company.

Know what makes really good products. To have the most possible success as a home entrepreneur, you want to make sure you're not just selling any old product. You want to make sure you're selling awesome products — products that are convenient, portable, and cheap to manufacture.

What makes a home product really good:

- Convenience. Your product makes life easier for your customers

- Portability. It ships easily. That also usually means it's easier to manufacture.

- Cost. It doesn't take an arm and a leg to manufacture. Try to get your margins at or above 50%.

What makes a home product not so good:

- Overly mechanical and liability-prone. If your product demands super high quality standards or puts you at a liability, stay away. No mechanical drills.

- Imported by big retailers. If the product you're trying to sell at home already is being sold at Walmart, don't expect much.

- Trademarks. Unless you want to spend all your profit fighting legal battles with huge corporations, stay away from items that are protected under trademark.

Start making your product. Very few retailers successfully buy wholesale and then flip the product(s) without changing it in some significant way. What you'll probably find yourself doing is buying the raw materials from a supplier or host of suppliers and then spending time and manpower fashioning your product into reality.

Slowly but surely, start to sell bigger and better. If you're serious about making money, you'll want to look at your sales after a couple months and figure out how to increase them.

CONCLUSION

Running your own business is a stressful but good career and life choice. It demands your time and focus. Start by expecting to live your work until it is established, so it can get off the ground. There are many different opinions about how to start a business.

Creating and sustaining your own business isn't just a way to wealth - it's a way to pursue your life's dreams and find personal fulfillment. This path isn't an easy one, but it's one that all of history's greatest entrepreneurs have had to follow. Though starting a business is easier if you have vast reserves of cash, it's possible to build a successful business from the ground, up with smarts, perseverance, and dedication even if you aren't loaded. If you're prepared to work hard and learn from your failures, you have the once-in-a-lifetime chance of building a successful business you can proudly call your own.

Do all things in moderation. Live life with a sense of balance, even when you're starting a business with barely a cent in the bank. Losing your perspective in life will make you poorer in the long run (emotionally - not necessarily financially), so it's never a risk worth taking. Never miss a night's sleep. Don't work yourself to death. Always devote time to your family, your hobbies, and, of course, yourself. Your life should be a source of joy and passion - not just an opportunity to work.

Additionally, you should never rely on drugs to aid your performance ability or to replace your regular healthy eating and exercise plans. This will, in the long run, break you down and cause you to make irrational, emotional decisions which are never a good thing in business.

www.ingramcontent.com/pod-product-compliance
Lightning Source LLC
Chambersburg PA
CBHW061446180526
45170CB00004B/1574